THE US PRESIDENT WHO SERVED LONGER THAN ANY OTHER PRESIDENT

BIOGRAPHY OF FRANKLIN ROOSEVELT CHILDREN'S BIOGRAPHY BOOK

Franklin Delano Roosevelt
32nd President of the United States

Franklin D. Roosevelt became the 32nd President of the United States in 1933 and served through 1945. He was born in Hyde Park, New York on January 30, 1882, and passed away in Warm Springs, Georgia on April 12, 1945. His vice-presidents were John Nance Garner (1933–1941), Henry A. Wallace (1941–1945), Harry S. Truman (1945).

In addition to serving four terms, he was the first president that had a significant physical disability. In 1921, at the age of 39, he was diagnosed with polio, also known as infantile paralysis.

He also went by the nickname FDR.

Read further to learn more about his journey through life.

WHAT ARE PRESIDENT ROOSEVELT'S GREATEST ACCOMPLISHMENTS?

He is known for commanding the United States and Allied Powers against the Axis Powers of Japan and German during World War II. He was also the leader of our country at the time of the Great Depression, establishing the New Deal, including the Federal Deposition Insurance Corporation (FDIC) and Social Security.

He held the office of president for four terms, two terms longer than any other president.

Franklin D. Roosevelt in 1900, at the age of 18.

HIS EARLY LIFE

He was born on a big estate near Hyde Park, New York, the only child of affluent parents, James and Sara Delano Roosevelt. His education was by tutors and elite schools such as Groton and Harvard. He started to admire and rival Theodore Roosevelt, his fifth cousin, who was elected to the presidency in 1900

Franklin Delano Roosevelt with father James Roosevelt in 1895

He fell in love with his distant cousin who was the niece of his rival. He then married Anna Eleanor Roosevelt in 1905. They produced a daughter named Anna, and five boys, James, Elliot, Franklin, John, and one who died at infancy.

Eleanor Roosevelt wearing her wedding dress in New York City, 1905

He went on to attend Columbia University, studying law, and then began working at a Wall Street law firm as a clerk for a few years. He proceeded to enter politics in 1910, winning a Democratic state senate seat in a deeply Republican Dutchess County.

Franklin D. Roosevelt in Cambridge, Massachusetts, 1904

President Woodrow Wilson named him the secretary of the United States Navy in 1913. He held that post for seven years and in 1918 traveled to Europe touring battlefields and naval bases after our country entered World War II.

Franklin D. Roosevelt as Assistant Secretary of the Navy. 1913.

BEFORE HIS PRESIDENCY

With support from his wife and of the journalist, Louis Howe, who had been a supporter of his for a long time, he started returning to life in the public eye, releasing statements regarding the issues for the day and keeping current correspondence with the Democratic leaders. His wife would speak publicly throughout the state of New York, making sure that FDR's reputation was strong, in spite of his illness.

Franklin D. Roosevelt with wife Eleanor Roosevelt

In addition, she organized the Democratic Party's women's division. FDR then made a triumphant appearance in 1924 at the Democratic National Convention when he nominated New York's Governor Alfred E. Smith for president. However, Smith lost this nomination and the Democrats went on to lose the general election.

Eleanor Roosevelt and Clementine Churchill at Quebec, Canada

CBC
CBC

In 1928, he again nominated Smith. This time Smith was successful and urged FDR to run for governor of New York. Smith then lost the election to Herbert Hoover, and Roosevelt won the election becoming the Governor of New York. Governor Roosevelt became more liberal with the policies while New York, as well as the nation, fell deep into an economic depression after the infamous 1929 stock market crash.

He started TERA, the Temporary Emergency Relief Administration, aiming to find work for those that were unemployed. By 1932, TERA was assisting about one of every 10 families throughout New York.

North Dakota

TER POINT
OOSEVELT
BYRNES
TED US UP
CHERAW
No 1
BYRNES
ROOSEVELT'S
FRIEND
JEFFERSON
FOR
ROOSEVELT
AND BYRNES
WHO GAVE US
A BREAK
WEXFORD
ROOSEVELT
& BYRNES
NEVER
LET US DOWN
ERFIE
SEVE
PAGELAND
FEELS SAFE
FOLLOWING
ROOSEVELT
AND
BYRNES
COU
BYR
COUR
WAN
D.
BAY
F
ROO
BY
THE
MIDDENDORF
100%
FOR THE
FARMERS
BROCK'S
MILL
FOR
ROOSEVELT
AND
BYRNES
GRANT'S
MILL
THE
NEW DEAL
LL KEEP
US SAF
PATRICK
ROOSEVELT
& BYRNES
OR BUST
SHILOH
ROOSEVELT
& BYRNE
DISPELLED
THE
PEE DEE
ROOSEVELT
BYRNES

Democratic Party campaign rally, Chesterfield County, South Carolina. 1936.
Signs support for Franklin Roosevelt and Senator James F. Burns.

FDR's PRESIDENCY

In 1930, he had been reelected as governor and became a front-runner as the Democratic presidential election in 1932. Breaking tradition, he accepted the nomination in Chicago in person, pledging himself as "a new deal for the American people".

Crowd in Cleveland to hear FDR's campaign speech. Nov. 3, 1940.
It was his final a speech before election day.

During the general election, exuberant and confident, he triumphed by a great margin over Hoover, who became known as a symbol for people during the Great Depression. Democrats also won a great majority in both the House of Representative and the Senate.

Signs for the 1936 election. Hardwick Vermont streets with campaign signs for 'Roosevelt and Garner', Sept. 1936.

ROOSEVELT AND GARNER
QUICK NATIONAL RECOVERY
PERMANENT
OLD AGE SECURITY
TOWNSEND PLAN
IT IS UP TO YOU TO
GET IT ENACTED INTO LAW
WORK FOR IT - VOTE FOR IT
LANDON KNOX
DRUG

Once he was inaugurated on March 4, 1933, the Depression had grown to despairing levels, which included as many as 13 million people unemployed.

The Great Depression. A row of out of work men at the New York City docks 1930s

During his first inaugural address, broadcast widely by radio, he boldly stated that *"This great nation will endure as it has endured, will revive and prosper. So, first of all, let me affirm my firm belief that the only we have to fear is fear itself"*.

CBS
MUTUAL

During his first 100 days, he closed all of the banks for a few days for Congress to pass legislation for reform. In addition, he started holding press conferences and regular radio broadcasts during which he would speak directly to America.

The first one of the "fireside chats", regarding the crisis in banking, went out to a radio audience of over 60 million and went a long way in restoring the public's confidence and stopping the harmful bank runs. After the Emergency Banking Relief Act was passed, three out of four back reopened within the week.

THE NEW DEAL

Once he became president, he first signed several new bills into laws in order to stop the Great Depression. These laws included the FDIC, Social Security, the Civilian Conservation Corps, new power plants, aid for farmers, and laws for improvement of working conditions. He then created the Security and Exchange Commission (SEC) for regulation of the stock market and to prevent future collapse of the financial markets.

Men during the great depression on the street during a bank run

WORLD WAR II

FDR warned America's public about the possible dangers of the hard-line regimes in Japan, Italy, and Germany around 1937, but did not go as far as to suggest that America abandon their isolationist policy. Once WWII began in September of 1939, he requested a special session of Congress to revise America's current neutrality acts and allowed for France and Britain to buy American arms on a "cash-and-carry" basis.

Franklin D. Roosevelt signing the declaration of war against Japan.

418
1000
220
220
1415
1175
1265
049

Near the end of June 1940, Germany was able to capture France and he convinced Congress to give Britain additional support, which was now on its own to fight the Nazi menace. Even though it was tradition that presidents only serve as president for two turns, he decided to run again in 1940 and defeated Wendell L Wilkie by almost 5 million votes.

Landing craft of with supply of U.S. forces on Okinawa, 13 days after the initial invasion.

With the passage of the Lend-Lease Act in March of 1941, Roosevelt was able to increase support of Great Britain and then had a meeting with Prime Minister Winston Churchill in August on board a battleship which was anchored off the coast of Canada.

"KEEP 'EM FLYING"
MBS
BS
NBC

This resulted in the Atlantic Charter, in which these two leaders declared the "Four Freedoms" on which they felt the post-war world be founded: freedom from fear, freedom from want, freedom of religion and freedom of speech and expression.

Franklin D. Roosevelt and Winston Churchill

Then, December 8, 1941, the day after Japan bombed Pearl Harbor, the U.S. naval base, he appeared in front of a joint session of Congress, and declared war on Japan. As the first president to leave our country at wartime, he started the alliance between countries that were combating the Axis, he met frequently with Churchill as well as seeking to create friendly relations with the Soviet Union, as well as its leader, Joseph Stalin.

FDR with Winston Churchill, L. McCarthy, King, Halifax and Soong in Washington, D.C

NBC
NBC
ABC

In the meantime, he constantly spoke on the radio, reporting on events of the war and rallying America and supporting the war effort.

Franklin D. Roosevelt on the air

From left to right:
Joseph Stalin,
Franklin D. Roosevelt
and Winston Churchill

THE YALTA CONFERENCE AND FDR's DEATH

As the war turned toward the Allies in 1944, he became ailing and weary but managed to win a fourth term as president. He then had a meeting with Churchill and Stalin the following February at the Yalta Conference. Roosevelt was able to get Stalin to commit to enter into the war against Japan after Germany's surrender.

Winston Churchill, Franklin D. Roosevelt and Joseph Stalin at the Yalta Conference

Stalin kept the promise, but did not honor his promise to create democratic governments in the eastern European nation which were under Soviet control at that time. The "Big Three" then worked building foundations for a post-war international peace organization which came to be known as the United Nations.

Franklin D. Roosevelt speaking with King Ibn Saud of Saudi Arabia at Great Bitter Lake in Egypt

When he returned from the Yalta conference, he was becoming so weak he had to sit while addressing Congress. Roosevelt left Washington early in April of 1945 and went to his home in War Springs, Georgia, where he had previously set up a nonprofit foundation that provided aid to patients with polio.

Franklin D. Roosevelt funeral in Hyde Park

He suffered a cerebral hemorrhage on April 12, 1945 and passed away later that same day. He was succeeded in office by vice-president, Harry S. Truman.

For additional information about President Roosevelt research the internet, go to your local library, and ask questions of your teachers, family, and friends.

Visit
BABY PROFESSOR
EDUCATION KIDS
www.BabyProfessorBooks.com
to download Free Baby Professor eBooks
and view our catalog of new and exciting
Children's Books